Identifying Antique Paperweights
Millefiori

Identifying
Antique
Paperweights
Millefiori

George N. Kulles

PAPERWEIGHT PRESS
SANTA CRUZ • CALIFORNIA

Dedicated to my wife, Jean,
without whose help and encouragement
this guide would not have been completed

Designed by Linda Marcetti

Copyright © 1985 by Paperweight Press

Second printing 1987

Library of Congress Cataloging in Publication Data

Kulles, George N.
    Identifying antique paperweights: millefiori

    Bibliography: p.
    1. Millefiori canes (Paperweights)
    2. Paperweights—History—19th century.
    3. Paperweights— Themes, motives. I. Title
NK 5440.P3K87   1987   748.8'4'09034   87-2278
ISBN 0-933756-07-0

Contents

Preface

Here is the indispensable guide for collectors of antique paper-weights. *Identifying Antique Paperweights—Millefiori* will be a delight to anyone interested in the subtle variations and distinctions to be found in these intricate and beautiful products of the glass-maker's art.

From his vantage point as a restorer and polisher of paperweights, George Kulles has been placed in the fortunate position of being able to examine countless weights. Now, for the benefit of collectors, he has organized his knowledge between the covers of this small but significant volume in a way that will simplify the task of recognizing and identifying the characteristics of all the major nineteenth-century producers.

While I have known George professionally for perhaps a decade, it was during the 1978 Corning Museum seminar on paperweights, where he gave a lecture on the identification of millefiori canes, that we both realized the need for a reference book on the subject. I encouraged him to continue his research, and offered to publish the book when it was ready; the final result has far exceeded my expectations.

Since this book deals primarily with identification, a few historical notes are in order. The techniques of combining different colors of glass to produce various designs can be traced back to ancient Egyptian workers, who made a variety of decorative and functional objects incorporating patterns fused directly into the glass. As these techniques were passed on and improved through centuries of experience they were perfected and refined, and a high state of proficiency had been reached by the beginning of the nineteenth century. The French factories, especially, produced many beautiful objects using millefiori canes, lampworked flowers, and other motifs encased in clear glass.

Around 1840 the idea of making a paperweight from glass occurred to someone; during the next twenty years the idea caught fire with French makers, and they competed with each other during this period to develop the most beautiful and unusual designs imaginable. Flowers of all sorts, reptiles, butterflies, and many other imitations of nature were made; but perhaps the most universal practice was the production of millefiori canes and the arrangement of them in abstract patterns within clear crystal paperweights.

The art of making paperweights spread to other European countries, mainly England and Italy, and to America. Toward the end of the nineteenth century production declined, and it was not until the 1950s that a strong interest in making and collecting paperweights was revived. Individual artists and factories began once more to produce paperweights in the classic French style, and also began inventing new designs and techniques.

During the period when paperweights were first produced, many people found satisfaction in collecting them. Today, interest in collecting has grown dramatically, and collectors all over the world are discovering the beauty of these small but brilliant objects of multi-colored glass. Paperweights also offer an excellent investment opportunity, and their value has increased consistently over the past thirty years as the interest in art objects made of glass has increased.

In attempting to establish the origin and authenticity of an antique weight, one should seek the advice of an expert;

however, much can be learned by becoming familiar with reference works and specialized books in the field. More and more books are becoming available today, but this is the first to focus on the identification of antique weights. It is therefore a major contribution to the literature about paperweights, and will be invaluable to all serious collectors.

Lawrence H. Selman
Santa Cruz, California
April 1985

Introduction

This guide has been written to help the enthusiast and beginning collector identify nineteenth-century paperweights from the major glass factories. It points out the subtle distinctions in areas such as rod design, depth of basal concavity, or twist of glass ribbons that, to the collector, make one paperweight as different from another as one person's face is from another.

The first section of this guide will help you identify the geometric rod and cane patterns that are the main design elements of the weights. Here, for example, you will find the information not only to identify the cane in your weight as a honeycomb but also to decide which of five manufacturers created this particular honeycomb.

The second section of this guide treats the non-geometric canes, that is, the silhouette and picture canes. For quick reference, a table has been included that identifies commonly found subjects with the manufacturers who favored them.

The third section lists clues, other than the basic internal design, that can help you identify or confirm your identification of an antique weight. Explanations are included on how to recognize spurious and genuine dates, initials that serve as signatures, and paperweight profiles typical of certain manufacturers.

Numerals in square brackets, thus: [14] refer to illustrations in the color plate section in the center of the book. Capital letters in brackets [A] refer to the bibliography at the end of the book.

Naturally, this guide is not and cannot be complete, as unique and exceptional antique paperweights are perhaps even now coming to light. It is based, rather, on a careful selection of the most helpful as well as the more commonly encountered elements that have been observed by the writer. For many of the facts in this guide, I wish to acknowledge my indebtedness to all those who have made their work available to our common interest: Yvette Amic, Percy Boore, Evangeline Bergstrom, Paul Hollister, Roger Imbert, Paul Jokelson, and Lawrence Selman; the contributors to thirty years of PCA Bulletins; and all the others who have searched out the many mysteries of these masterpieces of the glassmaker's art.

George N. Kulles
Lockport, Illinois
April 1985

1

Clues in Geometric Rods and Canes

To the casual observer, nineteenth-century millefiori canes appear quite similar. At first, their circles, stars, crosses, and squares might seem to yield few clues to paperweight identification. However, to the knowledgeable collector, the delicate distinctions in these simple forms make it clear that one weight is an antique Saint Louis while another is from Clichy.

This section of this book will explain how to distinguish among the fourteen types of nineteenth-century rods and canes that are the basic design elements in the majority of antique paperweights. To help you with your identification, both simple line drawings of the typical rods and canes and also photographs of actual weights containing these elements have been included.

Of course, these rod and cane configurations are not the only ones that occur in antique weights, nor are the glass factories mentioned in the text the only ones at which these rod forms were used; however, this guide attempts to identify the design elements you are most likely to encounter in antique paperweights and the factories that were prominent in the production of these weights.

Stars with Six Points

Six-point stars may be found in the paperweights of Baccarat, Clichy, Islington, Saint Louis, and Bohemia. Although there are some similarities among the stars of these companies, there are, however, many easily recognizable differences that can help you identify their manufacturers.

The Clichy star points have long straight sides with slightly tapered points. This star has a smaller center than any of the other canes depicted here. [48]

A second Clichy star has long arms with rounded tips [38] and closely resembles those from Islington Glass Works. [53]

The Saint Louis star has curved petal-like arms which end in points. [73]

Because the points of Bohemian stars are wide and short, their central bodies appear to be larger than those of other stars. Although usually sharply pointed, these stars occasionally have rounded points. [30]

The small additional points which appear at the convergence of each of the six large arms of the Baccarat example are exclusive to this glass house. When the star is large, these additional points are quite pronounced. In smaller stars they are minute extrusions which can usually be seen with the aid of a magnifying lens. [13]

There is also a rarely encountered Saint Louis twelve point star that slightly resembles the Baccarat form described above. Whereas the six large Baccarat points are thick in outline, the Saint Louis points are long thin spikes.

Irregularly Shaped Leaves

Irregularly shaped leaves that occur only in Baccarat paperweights are small, opaque, white boat-shaped rods filled with translucent green glass. They are used primarily as an element in complex canes, where they seldom retain their original outline but instead are contorted, crushed or turned awry.

The first drawing shows the basic shape of the rod; the second depicts the distorted shapes that are frequently found; the last figure shows a complex cane with seven irregularly shaped leaves, typically askew. [7]

Honeycombs

Honeycomb canes were produced by five factories—Baccarat, Saint Louis, Islington, Clichy and Bacchus.

Baccarat frequently used the star honeycomb, a white or cream opaque glass plaque with star-shaped openings filled with golden yellow translucent glass. These openings contain the characteristic extra minute points of the Baccarat star. The star honeycomb is usually found at the center of lamp-worked flowers. [14]

Another variety made by Baccarat was a cane of round white tubes filled with translucent aqua glass. This honeycomb occurs as a bundled cane or as an element in a millefiori cane of greater complexity. [15]

Whereas the Baccarat honeycomb was made of bundled rods, a similar Saint Louis honeycomb was made as a single unit, a white plaque containing translucent blue openings. [65]

Unlike the Islington honeycomb which has crisp angles, those from Saint Louis are slightly rounded. There are two varieties of these complex canes: a cane of four honeycomb cells, [63] and a cane of nine cells. The latter cane usually has its center rod replaced by a small floret. [62]

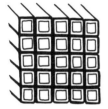

The rare Islington honeycomb cane of twenty-five square tubes is arranged in parallel rows of five and is compressed tightly into an almost square cane. [53]

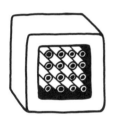

The honeycomb produced by the Clichy factory is also rare. Its opaque square frame encloses parallel rows of round honeycomb tubes, in various color combinations. It closely resembles a commercially packaged honeycomb. [40]

The Bacchus honeycomb rod is a white plaque with an outer row of six holes evenly spaced around a central opening. All seven holes are filled with translucent pink glass. [25]

Cog Canes

Most cog canes, sharply pointed or crenelated, look very much alike, with differences, when they do occur, in the number of teeth on their circumference. The most common ones, with six, eight, twelve and sixteen serrations, were manufactured by almost every paperweight factory and so are not useful as a means of identifying weights. However, there are examples that can provide reliable clues to their place of origin.

Number of teeth	Nineteenth-century company
5	Sandwich, New England Glass Company
7	Bacchus
9	Gillinder, Bacchus
10	Sandwich, New England Glass Company, Bacchus, Gillinder, Whitefriars
14	Saint Louis, Bacchus, Gillinder
15	Bacchus
18	Bacchus
20	Baccarat
22	Baccarat
28	Saint Louis

The fourteen cog rod is often found in Saint Louis paperweights. In this factory's carpet ground weights almost every cane contains fourteen cogs. In Saint Louis concentric paperweights, rings of millefiori often are made up of cane after cane with fourteen teeth. [66] Other factories where fourteen cog canes were occasionally used were Bacchus [26] and Gillinder. [50]

Saint Louis paperweights also frequently contain canes with twenty-eight points. Nearly all this manufacturer's silhouette or picture canes have twenty-eight teeth on their edges. [69]

Like other companies, Baccarat made canes with six, eight, and twelve teeth, but it appears to have been the only one that made twenty and twenty-two cog canes. Thus, paperweights containing rods with twenty or twenty-two teeth can be almost certainly identified as products of the Baccarat factory. [16, 17]

The Boston & Sandwich Company and the New England Glass Company made many rods with five and ten cogs. Because Bacchus, Whitefriars and Gillinder also produced ten cog rods, you can generally assume that if an antique weight contains a ten-point cane, it was made in either an American or British factory. [50, 54]

A collector will also occasionally encounter seven, fifteen, and eighteen cog canes in weights from Bacchus, [24] and nine cog canes in weights from both Gillinder and Bacchus.

Lobed Canes

Rods with three and four lobes are found in Baccarat, Islington, and Bohemian paperweights. Those made at Baccarat and Islington are rounded; those from Bohemia are pointed, with design elements reminiscent of the patterns on early cased Bohemian cut glass.

The Baccarat trefoil is a three-lobed white tube usually filled with red glass. It is a common rod in Baccarat close packed millefiori weights, found in a bundled cane or as an element in a very complex cane. [11]

The quatrefoil from Baccarat has four round lobes outlined in white and filled with dark green, red, or turquoise glass. Like the trefoil, it was used in the construction of intricate canes. [18]

The Baccarat shamrock, a green three-lobed rod with a stem, resembles the typical Irish shamrock. The tip of each leaf is often slightly indented. [17]

The Islington Glass Works propeller-shaped rod has three projecting arms. Its lobes are less rounded and appear longer than those of the Baccarat trefoil. [52]

The Bohemian trefoil resembles the hepatica leaf with three pointed lobes and a stem. [34]

Florets

Although there are many more types of florets (flower-like canes) in antique paperweights than those depicted here, these are some representative examples.

This first floret is from Saint Louis. It has a red, green, or blue hexagonal center with concave sides. A round white petal surrounds each of the six points of the hexagon. [61]

The next tiny Saint Louis flower is very much like the first but is altered by a layer of colored glass crimped on the border of the flower. The crimping has turned the edges of the round white petals into random points, creating a beautiful variation of the original. [67]

Most Clichy florets were made with six or eight petals, usually with a prominent red or blue dot at their centers. They may be found singly or as a part of a more complex cane, as when they were used as the centers of Clichy moss canes. [43]

The Clichy edelweiss floret resembles the small Alpine flower. The puffy contour of the white cane contrasts with the characteristically crisp shape of most Clichy canes. [39]

New England Glass Company florets are fuller bodied than the common floret from Clichy, and have very short petals. [57]

Arrows and Anchors

Arrow and anchor rods were made by Baccarat, Saint Louis, Clichy, Bohemia, and Islington.

The Baccarat arrow rod (also "crow's foot" rod) usually has ruler perfect lines, all three converging in a sharp point. When arrows are found in complex canes surrounding and pointing to a central rod, the millefiori design is known as an arrowhead cane. [23]

The point of the Saint Louis rod is slightly rounded, hence it is called an "anchor". Saint Louis anchors are not as carefully placed in "anchorhead" canes as the rods in the Baccarat arrowhead canes. Whereas Baccarat arrows usually point to dead center, Saint Louis anchors aim at all directions of the compass. [64]

Arrow rods made at Clichy resemble the straight Baccarat arrow but have a short thick-set design. [49]

Because many Bohemian arrows appear to run off the edge of the rod, they lack a definite point. The Bohemian arrow has long wedge-shaped lines that grow narrower as the distance from their non-existent point increases. [33]

The Islington arrow is short and stubby, resembling the Clichy example, but usually has a point that runs off the edge of the rod. [52]

Matchhead Centers

The Saint Louis factory produced small-domed opaque flower centers that resemble the tips of wooden matches. The small flowers with match head centers appear in flat and up-right bouquets. Most of the centers are yellow in color, but may be red, blue, or green.

Baccarat also made flowers with match head centers for a few bouquets. These centers, which were sparingly used, appeared in a variety of colors and were slightly longer than the ones made by Saint Louis.

Whorls

Whorl and concentric circle canes were made by many nineteenth-century paperweight companies. Because the bull's-eye or concentric circle cane was relatively easy to produce, it was universally used, thereby making it nearly useless as a means of identifying weights. The whorl, however, required more complex manufacturing techniques and was, therefore, less common. It is most frequently found in Baccarat close packed millefiori and choufleur carpet ground weights. However, it also made a fleeting appearance in a few early Saint Louis paperweights and in the few positively identified Islington paperweights.

The Baccarat whorl begins at the center of the rod with a small circle. It then coils around itself either clockwise or counterclockwise and terminates in an open-ended flap. Baccarat whorls were used singly as canes, used as component parts of complex designs, or bundled together into a complex motif. [21]

Unlike the Baccarat whorl which begins with a small circle at its center, the early Saint Louis whorl starts with a line that coils about itself, ending in a flap.

The coil of the Islington whorl is small and thick, with only a few turns in its configuration and no beginning circle at its center. [52]

Crosses

Several glassworks have used rods with a cruciform design.

Baccarat produced the fortress cane, so called because, with imagination, one can picture a diamond-shaped castle with four concave sides at the cane's center. Each of the four sharp corners of this fortress has a small round turret connected by an outer wall. [12]

The large Saint Louis cross cane also has a diamond shape at its center. Each surrounding layer of glass softens the sharp points of the central diamond. The outer layer is shaped so that each point terminates in a broad rounded foot, giving the cane the appearance of a Jerusalem cross. [71]

Another Saint Louis cross occurs in very early weights. The rods are small, round, and white and have thick blue or red crosses with bulbous ends. [65]

Bacchus and New England Glass Company cruciform rods are thick and even-armed with each branch ending in a broad triangular shape. [28, 58]

Bacchus also made another cross, which is white and thick and has arms of equal length. At the center of this cross is a black octagonal shape, with a white rod in its center. This Bacchus cross is enclosed in a thin white tube. [27]

The crosses found in Bohemian and Clichy weights have four short, thick arms of equal length. [42]

The Islington cross resembles those of Bohemia and Clichy but has a slightly thinner outline.

The Venetian cross has double-pointed arms, similar to a Maltese cross.

Pastry Mold Canes

Clichy's pastry mold canes are beautiful and very plentiful. Their tops measure half the diameter of their bases, and their sides are marked by deep ribbon-like folds. [41]

Although stretched and cut into disks like other millefiori canes, these canes were prepared and placed into paperweights so that their sides billowed out, causing their surface area to increase four-fold. The color of the flared-out edge of the pastry mold cane became the cane's dominant color. The Clichy cone-spreading technique, created intentionally or discovered accidentally, became one of Clichy's recurring hallmarks.

Roses

Almost every paperweight glass house has fashioned rose canes during the past 130 years. [B] Below are some typical roses from four nineteenth-century sources—Clichy, Baccarat, Bohemian, and the Boston & Sandwich Company.

Most Clichy roses are of three types, although there are other earlier and rarer varieties, which have not been included here. In all types the rose petals are usually pink but may also be blue, white, purple, green, or yellow.

Clichy Type I has a large central rod surrounded by one row of small white or yellow stamen rods. The flower petals, single platelets or flattened tubes, surround the stamen. The outer sheath of the cane has platelets, usually of a contrasting color, representing the flower's sepals. [35]

Clichy Type II has a central pistil surrounded by two rings of stamens. [36]

Type III has a bundle of rods at the center. [37]

The Baccarat rose is vibrant salmon pink and has star rods representing the pistil and stamens. [6]

Bohemian factories made several varieties of the rose cane, the most common a true cabbage rose. Its petals are slightly ruffled and spaced further apart than those of Clichy or Baccarat. [29]

The Nicholas Lutz rose from the Boston & Sandwich Company has a central dollop of murky red glass surrounded by thick slabs of opaque white that represent rose petals. The sepals in the outer sheath are coated with translucent green glass. [74]

Rod Bundles

Baccarat and Clichy bundled rods together for a variety of uses. One well-known example of a rod bundle is the moss cane from Clichy, which may or may not have a floret at the center. The individual round white moss cane rods are crimped with an outer layer of translucent green glass; it is this layer that gives a bed of these canes the appearance of green moss. [48]

Plain Clichy rod bundles are sometimes found as centers of Type III rose canes and more frequently as centers of pastry mold canes.

 Baccarat bundles are comprised of six-point star rods. These bundled star rods appear in rose canes, in close packed millefiori paperweights, and as centers for lampworked flowers. [1]

Split Millefiori Flower Petals

The use of individual millefiori canes as simple flowers or as parts of more complex flowers was a standard practice in most factories. However, Clichy seems to be the only company that split lengths of cane vertically and utilized the exposed faces of the split cylinder as flower petals. Although beautiful blossoms were created with these slices, relatively only a few were produced.

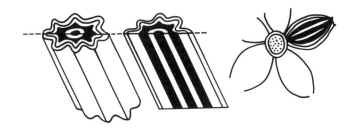

2

Silhouette and Picture Canes

Antique paperweights occasionally have canes that contain charming miniature silhouettes or colorful pictures. Some of these tiny subjects were exclusively used by a single glass house; other subjects, although differing in execution, can be found in weights by several companies.

True silhouettes were constructed in pre-shaped molds. The dark glass was formed to the desired shape and then encased in a contrasting color. Reverse silhouettes were made in opaque white glass and then enclosed within a darker color. In rare instances, it is possible to find two silhouettes in one cane—for example, in a Saint Louis weight in which a dog cane is combined with a devil cane. [60]

Once in a great while silhouette canes made at one company have found their way into paperweights made at another company. One occasionally sees a New England Glass Company paperweight that, although perfect in other details, contains a cane that has seemingly cracked or exploded. A close inspection of the weight will reveal a distorted or collapsed Bohemian silhouette cane inside, apparently the result of the incompatibility of the glasses used by the two factories. Extremely rare is the Baccarat silhouette in a Clichy weight, although I have seen two examples of this myself. In these weights, due to the incompatibility of the glass, the silhouette canes became slightly distorted during the annealing process. This example shows a somewhat distorted Baccarat pelican at the center of a Clichy cane. [46] Compare it to the photograph which shows the pelican silhouette in a Baccarat weight. [5]

Unlike silhouette canes, picture canes were constructed with many carefully shaped pieces of colored glass. These were combined in such designs as flowers and portraits and then fused to form large canes. Like geometric millefiori canes, large picture canes, after their initial construction, were reheated and stretched into long thin rods. They were then cut into hundreds of disks, each a miniaturized replica of the original design.

The following is a list of picture and silhouette cane subjects that were used by eight nineteenth-century glass houses. Where the same subject was used by more than one company, I have included brief descriptions to aid you in making your identification. Be aware that although the list contains most of the antique subjects known to the writer, other varieties undoubtedly exist—rare designs and variations are continuously discovered. [C]

ANTEATER

*(also identified as
a profile of Punch)*

Saint Louis

BEE

Bohemian—fat body
with two sets of horizontal lines across the body

Sandwich/NEGC—long,
thin body with one set of
horizontal lines [57]

BIRD

Venetian—elongated
neck [78]

BIRDS *(two)*

Venetian—with white
eyes [76]

Baccarat—facing each
other

BRIDGE *(railway)*

Venetian [77]

BUTTERFLY

(also identified as a moth)

Baccarat—single wing on each side of a thin body

NEGC—double wing on each side of a thick body

CAMEL

Saint Louis [69]

CHECKERBOARD

Venetian [77]

CLOVER

Baccarat [17]

DANCING COUPLE

Saint Louis—two girls or a boy and a girl [66]

DANCING DEVIL

Saint Louis—long curved back with short trousered legs and a tail [61]

DANCING DEVILS *(two)*

Saint Louis—long curved backs with short trousered legs and tails

Bohemian—faun-like legs

DANCING GIRL

Saint Louis

DANCING MAN

Saint Louis—with rod across his shoulders [70]

Saint Louis—with arms out to his sides

DEER

Baccarat [21]

DEVIL

Baccarat—crouching frontal view

Bohemian—faun-like legs

Saint Louis—running, in profile, long curved back with short trousered legs and a tail [61]

Saint Louis—running, in profile, thin branchlike body [60]

Venetian—running, in profile, in a full frock coat, with one arm extended

DOG

Baccarat—tail thick and curved upward [9]

COLOR PLATES

BACCARAT

1 / bundled rods

2 / twists

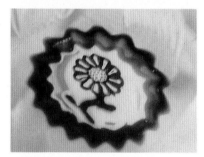

3 / flower

4 / goat

5 / pelican

6 / rose

7 / irregular leaves

8 / rooster

9 / dog

10 / horse

11 / trefoil

12 / fortress, squirrel

13 / 6 point stars

14 / star honeycomb

15 / honeycomb

BACCARAT (continued)

16 / 20 cog

17 / 22 cog, shamrock

18 / quatrefoil

19 / monkey

20 / date, signature

21 / deer, whorl

22 / elephant

23 / arrow

BACCHUS

24 / 18 cog, profile

25 / honeycomb

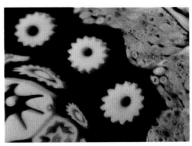

26 / 14 cog

27 / cross

28 / cross

BOHEMIAN

29 / rose

30 / 6 point stars

BOHEMIAN *(continued)*

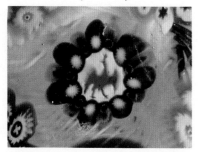

31 / eagle

32 / dog, monkey, rabbit

33 / arrow

34 / trefoil

CLICHY

35 / Type I rose

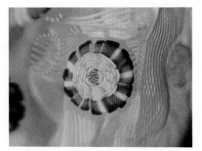

36 / Type II rose

37 / Type III rose

38 / 6 point stars

39 / edelweiss

40 / honeycomb

41 / pastry mold

42 / cross

43 / floret

44 / muslin — top view

45 / muslin — bottom view

CLICHY *(continued)*

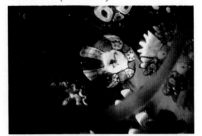

46 / Baccarat silhouette

47 / signature

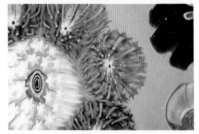

48 / 6 point stars, bundled rods

49 / arrow

GILLINDER

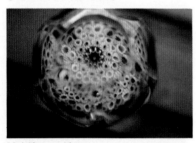

50 / 10 cog, 14 cog

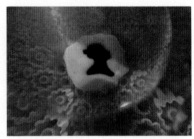

51 / profile

ISLINGTON

52 / arrow, propeller, whorl, signature

53 / 6 point stars, honeycomb

NEW ENGLAND
GLASS COMPANY

54 / 5 cog, 10 cog

55 / rabbit

56 / date

57 / floret, bee

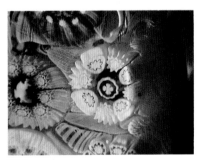

58 / cross

SAINT LOUIS

59 / twists

SAINT LOUIS *(continued)*

60 / double silhouette: dog, thin devil

61 / floret, dancing devil

62 / 9 cell honeycomb

63 / 4 cell honeycomb, date, signature

64 / arrow or anchor

65 / cross, honeycomb

66 / 14 cog, 2 dancing girls

67 / floret

68 / crown

69 / 28 cog, camel

70 / dancing man with rod

71 / cross

72 / flower

73 / 6 point stars

SANDWICH

74 / rose

VENETIAN

75 / gondola, portraits

76 / 2 birds, date

77 / bridge, checkerboard

78 / bird

79 / serifed letter

Bohemian—thick stalk-like legs [32]

Saint Louis—thick body, slender upward curving tail

Saint Louis—shaggy white dog [60]

Venetian—sitting dog

DOVE

(also identified as a pigeon)
Baccarat

DUCK WITH DUCKLINGS

Saint Louis

EAGLE

Bohemian—with long neck [31]

NEGC/Sandwich—with short neck

Venetian—double-headed eagle

ELEPHANT

Baccarat [22]

FLOWER *(single)*

Baccarat—several varieties [3]

Saint Louis—usually in a 28 cog cane [72]

Venetian—pansy

FLOWERS *(multiple)*

Baccarat

GOAT

Baccarat—with four legs showing [4]

Venetian—with two legs showing

GONDOLA

Venetian [75]

HEART

Sandwich/NEGC

HORSE *(four legs showing)*

Baccarat—close cropped tail [10]

Saint Louis—erect head, long-legged and sleek

Bohemian—both front legs extended

Islington—draft horse with upraised front leg

HORSE *(two legs showing)*

Venetian

LYRE

Venetian

MAN ON HORSE

NEGC/Sandwich

MAN WITH RIFLE

Baccarat

MONKEY

Baccarat—black, with two legs, bent at knees, and tail that curves down

Baccarat—white, with one leg, bent at knee, and tail that curves up [19]

Bohemian—a short body, with two straight legs, short straight tail [32]

MOON

Venetian—profile of man-in-the-moon

MOTH

(also identified as a butterfly)

Baccarat—single wing on each side of a thin body

NEGC—wings in four sections, thick body

NEGRO

Venetian—frontal view of full-length figure in striped trousers

OWL

Venetian—holding two tablets

PELICAN

Baccarat—head bent down [5]

Venetian—head erect

PHEASANT

Baccarat

PIGEON

(also identified as a dove)

Baccarat

PUNCH

(also identified as an anteater)

Saint Louis

PORTRAIT CANES

Venetian [75]

RABBIT

Bohemian—running, long full ears, sometimes has a red eye [32]

NEGC/Sandwich—running, short ears [55]

Whitefriars—sitting, in profile

RAILWAY BRIDGE

Venetian [77]

ROOSTER

Baccarat [8]

ROSEBUSH

Venetian—green foliage with red dots

SHAMROCK

Baccarat [17]

SQUIRREL

Baccarat [12]

STORK

Baccarat

SWAN

Baccarat

TURKEY

Saint Louis

WOMAN'S HEAD IN PROFILE

Gillinder—same silhouette as Bacchus [51]

Bacchus—same silhouette as Gillinder [24]

3

General Clues
in Paperweights

There are several other distinguishing characteristics that
can help you identify paperweights, though some are admit-
tedly of less value than others. While you should not expect to
identify a paperweight on the basis of a single characteristic,
you should be able to make a more dependable identification
as you accumulate a number of these clues.

Dates

Certain dates in paperweights are reliable indicators of the
time and place of manufacture, whereas other dates are
spurious, included in twentieth-century weights to increase
their values. You are most likely to encounter the nineteenth-
century dates, both genuine and counterfeit, found on the
following list:

Date	Maker	Comments
1815	*Dupont*	Date is in a rectangular piece of white glass. Modern paperweight with a false date.
1825	*NEGC/Sandwich*	White numbers in blue rods. This is an antique weight probably made in the 1850's.

Date	Maker	Comments
1837	Dupont	Modern paperweight with a false date.
1845	Baccarat	Each number in a separate rod with rods fused together. Date is a combination of various colors. Antique weight.
	Saint Louis	Each number is a separate rod with rods fused together and with the letters "SL" above the date. Antique weight.
	Venetian	Two varieties exist: the first is the date in a serrated rectangular white rod; the second has the letters "POB" in the same cane with the date. Antique weight.
1846	Baccarat	Antique.
	Saint Louis	Antique.
	Venetian	Antique.
1847	Baccarat	Antique.
	Saint Louis	Antique.
	Venetian	Antique. [76]
1848	Baccarat	Antique. [20]
	Bohemian	Numerals in a single cane below a "J" letter cane. Antique.

Date	Maker	Comments
1848	Dupont	Date is in a rectangular piece of white glass. Modern paperweight with a false date.
	Saint Louis	Antique. [63]
	Whitefriars	Individual rods separated by clear glass. Antique.
1849	Baccarat	Antique.
1851	Dupont	Modern paperweight with a false date.
1852	Dupont	Date is in a rectangular piece of white glass. Modern paperweight with a false date.
	NEGC/Sandwich	White numbers in blue rods. Antique. [56]
1853	Baccarat	Antique.
1858	Baccarat	Antique.
1869	Murano	Date in script form on white plaque. Modern paperweight with a false date.
1885	Murano	Date on white plaque. Modern paperweight with a false date.

Signature Canes and Other Letter Canes

Company signature canes occasionally appear in antique paperweights, with or without an accompanying date.

The Baccarat signature, the letter "B" in red, blue, or green, almost always appears in a white rod. [20] When found with a date, the letter will be above and in contact with the date rods.

Clichy's signature appears in three script styles: straight serifs, curved serifs, and letters without serifs. The most common signature cane is the individual letter "C". [47] On rare occasions, portions of the name "CLICHY" appear in a weight. The rarest signatures are those in which the entire name "CLICHY" appears.

The signature cane of Islington Glass Works is a white plaque with the letters "IGW". [52]

The letter "J" used in some Bohemian weights probably identified the weight as having been produced at the Josephine Glass Works.

The Saint Louis signature "SL" occurs with or without a date. Both letters appear in a single cane. [63]

In antique Venetian weights, "POB" indicates that the weight was made by Pietro Bigaglia; paperweights made by G. B. Franchini were marked "GBF". In Venice letters were also used to personalize weights with people's initials or names, or to commemorate special events. [A] "FI" appears on the breast of a double-headed eagle silhouette cane, probably to honor the Austrian emperor Ferdinand *(Ferdinand Imperator)*. I have also seen, individually or in combination, these large serifed letters on square plaques: A, B, C, D, E, F, I, L, M, N, O, P, R, and W. [79] No doubt the rest of the alphabet has also appeared in Venetian weights.

Although it was not customary for Sandwich to include letters in their paperweights, there does exist one possibly unique weight containing a weed flower with a large "B" at the flower's center.

Filigree, Ribbons, and Cables

Observing the direction of the glass strands when an antique paperweight is held with its filigree, ribbons, or cables standing vertically, can also help you identify a paperweight. Filigree, ribbons, and cables occur in torsades, upset muslin grounds, snakes, crown weights, chequer weights, end-of-day weights, and others.

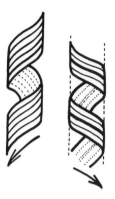

When the strands appear to descend to the left, the weight is Bohemian or Baccarat. [2]

If the strands twist down to the right, it is New England Glass Company, Sandwich, Saint Louis, [59] or Clichy.

Venetian and Val St. Lambert strands have twists in both directions, often intermixed in the same paperweight.

Exceptions to these rules do exist. For example, in a beautiful Saint Louis crown weight in the Bergstrom collection, the artist mirrored every third ribbon downward, to the left, a direction atypical of Saint Louis. [68]

Grounds

Although the majority of paperweight designs appear in clear glass, motifs were sometimes placed on ornate backgrounds. Paperweight factories had certain predilections for using some grounds and avoiding others. This chart shows the preferences of five nineteenth-century companies. [H]

Table of Ground Preferences

	Baccarat	Clichy	Saint Louis	Sandwich	NEGC
Color	rarely	occasionally	rarely	never	rarely
Jasper	rarely	never	occasionally	occasionally	rarely
Latticinio	never	occasionally	occasionally	occasionally	occasionally
Upset Muslin	occasionally	occasionally	rarely	never	rarely
Carpet	occasionally	occasionally	occasionally	rarely	occasionally
Sand	occasionally	never	never	never	never
Flash	rarely	never	occasionally	never	never

Saint Louis jasper ground weights often have a double gather of jasper. When the weight is observed through the basal concavity, a smaller jasper gather can be easily seen as a cushion within the larger outer bed of jasper.

In Clichy weights that have an upset muslin ground, the lower layer of filigree is usually laid in parallel strips.

When the bases of weights from Bohemia, Baccarat, Saint Louis, and New England Glass Company are examined, the muslin strands are all drawn to the center of the base.

In the photographs are five muslin ground paperweights from these companies, with the Clichy weight in the center. When the weights are inverted, the parallel strips of Clichy muslin are quite apparent. [44, 45]

Facets

Paperweight companies used specific patterns when faceting paperweights. However, you should be aware that over the years many paperweights have been modified or refaceted with atypical designs by independent glass cutters with little knowledge of the characteristic company patterns. Although other types of faceting exist, the designs here are those most often encountered. [G]

There are three common Baccarat faceting patterns. The first, the most common, has a printy (concave cut) on top and six printies around the side. The side windows are placed characteristically high, with their centers above the middle of the weight.

The next example, used on many overlay weights, has a top printy and six side windows. In addition, this variety has small oval cuts around the bottom edge of the weight.

This flat-cut Baccarat pattern was used primarily for large sulphides. These weights have a large facet on top and many rows of diamond-shaped facets covering the sides of the weights.

A common Clichy pattern had a large printy or facet on top and five or six large windows around the side. These side printies were placed with their centers at the mid-point of the weight.

Another pattern from Clichy has a large top printy and five or six small side printies. The side printies are interspaced with long, narrow vertical flutes.

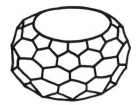

The first of four Saint Louis examples has a large window on top; the rest of the weight is covered with hexagonally shaped printies.

A common Saint Louis design has small square printies in parallel rows over the top of the weight. The side is cut with large windows.

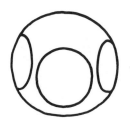

Another design from Saint Louis, usually found with dahlias on latticinio, has an uncut top and large printies around the side.

The last Saint Louis example has a medium-sized printy on top, surrounded by a row of seven or eight small printies. The sides are cut with an additional row of six large printies or two rows of smaller printies.

Gillinder weights are faceted with deep, long, oval-shaped printies that extend from the base to the top. These weights have a medium-sized printy on top.

A feature found in faceted New England Glass Company weights is a four-printy cut top, each window overlapping its neighbors. This produces a large four-petal, clover-shaped window. Various side cuttings were used with this design.

Basal Cuts

Most nineteenth-century paperweight houses sometimes cut decorative stars into their basal concavities.

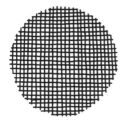

Clichy, also, on rare occasion, cut an extremely fine grid pattern in a paperweight base.

Another rare basal cut design unique to Clichy was the unusual pattern consisting of petal-like cuts alternating with long, sharp points.

Paperweight Profiles

Certain factors—the size of a motif, how the design was placed within the glass, the properties of the glass, and the manufacturing methods used—determined how each company chose the characteristic shape that would most effectively display its own motifs. Each, therefore, developed a basic shape which it used for the majority of its weights. Consequently, the profile of an unaltered paperweight can often help you identify it. [D]

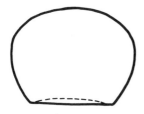

The Baccarat weights have a profile, medium in height, with a slightly flattened crown. The sides have a full curve that turns in at the base.

Saint Louis made weights with high profiles and well-rounded crowns. The sides are steep, gently curved, and turn in slightly at the base.

Those from Clichy have a medium profile with an almost perfectly rounded crown. The sides continue the line of the crown and curve well into the base. Occasionally one sees a Clichy weight with a "making mark," an indentation around the weight where the two halves were put together. Basal concavities are generally shallow.

Bacchus weights are generally large glass cushions with well-rounded domes and sides that have deep curves, going well into the base. The design is usually enclosed within a basket of cog canes drawn to the center of the base.

The weights with very high profiles and steep sides are from the New England Glass Company. The sides come down to the base in a slightly curved line. These weights often exhibit a complex basal ring, as the result of the residual edge of the design cushion being exposed as a secondary rim in the basal concavity. Basal concavities are deeply cut in these weights.

The profile of the early Whitefriars weights (dated 1848) resembles a large single convex lens. The motif, appearing on a low cushion, is covered with a thick layer of clear glass that gently curves to the base. Similar to that of the New England Glass Company weights, the typical Whitefriars base rests on the initial gather as well as on the ring of the enclosing dome.

Compared with other nineteenth-century paperweights, those from the Boston & Sandwich Company have an extremely low profile and a rather flat crown. The sides have a short deep curve that turns well into the base. Many of these weights contain a small surface irregularity at the center of the crown, as if the weight had not received a final finish with the shaping block.

Fluorescence

Fluorescence is the property in a paperweight that produces visible light waves when acted upon by the radiant energy of the short, invisible ultra-violet rays of black light. Experiments with black light have revealed that, depending on its composition, glass from various companies fluoresces in different colors.

In a major exhibition in 1978, a large number of paperweights were tested for fluorescence. [E] This testing produced the following information: 97% of 76 antique Baccarat weights fluoresced pale pink; 92% of 73 antique Saint Louis weights fluoresced coral pink; 89% of 75 Clichy weights fluoresced lime green. Because weights from other nineteenth-century makers were limited in number in this exhibition, and because the few that were available showed too wide a range of colors, their test results were too inconclusive to be included in this guide.

Many clues have been offered in this guide, yet the reader will occasionally find that an antique paperweight will defy identification. Unfortunately there are still a few unidentified paperweights as well as a number of weights with tentative attributions. Consequently, a need exists for additional research to uncover the clues necessary for their positive identification.

Even as this is being written, important knowledge is coming to light. Several years ago information was uncovered that suggests a possible Russian source of plaques and letter seals which were formerly identified as Mount Washington. More recently, a discovery in a French museum points to the Pantin

factory as the probable source of antique salamander paperweights and of certain "mystery" flower weights.

More work is certainly needed in many areas. Someone will
one day sort out the various Bohemian factories; better
guidelines will be developed for the provenance of perplexing
sulphides; a researcher will untangle the confusion in later
Baccarat weights; serious students of glass will eventually
make an in-depth exploration of transitional millefiori canes
that will tie in early prototype weights with those that contain
the more familiar characteristics of the major factories; others
may search out records of those nineteenth-century factories
alluded to by their contemporaries as having produced
paperweights. These areas, as well as others, await the efforts
of enthusiastic collectors and researchers. Everyone can and
should be involved, for shared knowledge enriches us all.

Glossary

Anchor rod. A millefiori section made from rods containing an anchor motif.

Annealing. Gradually reducing the temperature of the finished paperweight to insure even cooling and to prevent cracking.

Arrow rod. A millefiori section made from rods containing a three-pronged arrow motif.

Base. The bottom of a paperweight.

Basal ring. The ring around the bottom of a concave base where the paperweight comes into contact with the supporting surface.

Bouquet. A floral design composed of more than one flower.

Cable. See **twist.**

Cane. A cross-section of a molded or bundled glass rod that has been pulled out to miniaturize the interior design.

Carpet ground. An overall pattern of identical millefiori canes used as a backdrop for a motif.

Chequer weight. A paperweight in which the millefiori canes are separated by short lengths of latticinio twists in a checkerboard fashion.

Classic period. Paperweight production in France between 1840 and 1860.

Cog cane. A millefiori cane which has been molded with a serrated edge. This type of cane edge is quite common on silhouette canes.

Color ground. Opaque or transparent colored glass used as a background for a paperweight motif.

Concentric. General name for any spacing scheme in millefiori weights which features concentric circles of canes placed around a central cane or cluster of canes. Concentric weights are either "open" (circles spaced relatively far apart) "close" (circles close together), or "spaced" (millefiori canes set equal distances apart in vaguely defined concentric circles).

Crimped cane. Vertically ribbed or corrugated cane.

Crown (or **dome**). The glass in a paperweight which is above the motif.

Crown weight. A type of paperweight in which alternately colored and lacy white twisted bands radiate from a central cane near the top of the dome, flow down the sides of the weight, and converge again near the base.

Crowsfoot. See **arrow rod.**

Cushion. Ground on which the decorative element(s) of a paperweight rests. It is usually convex in appearance when viewed through the top or sides of the weight.

Cut (or **cutting**). Grinding the surface of a paperweight for ornament.

Date rod. A millefiori cane with numerals identifying the year of manufacture.

Dome. See **crown.**

End-of-day weight. See **scrambled millefiori.**

Facet (or **printy**). The level or concave surface formed when the side or top of a paperweight is shaped with a flat or rounded grinding wheel. (**Printy** usually refers to a concave facet.)

Filigree. See **lace.**

Flash. A thin coating of transparent glass applied to the base of a paperweight, or the entire weight in the case of a flash overlay.

Floret. A flower-like pattern within a cane.

Fluorescence. The property in a paperweight that produces visible light waves when acted upon by the radiant energy of the short, invisible ultraviolet rays of black light.

Flute (or **fluting**). A pattern of deep narrow grooves usually cut vertically on the outside of a paperweight.

Ground (or **color ground**). A cushion on which the decorative element of a paperweight rests.

Honeycomb. A type of millefiori cane, the cross-section of which resembles the cell pattern of a honeycomb.

Initial cane. See **signature cane.**

Jasper ground. Paperweight backdrop formed by a mixture of two colors of finely ground glass.

Lace (or **filigree, muslin,** or **upset muslin).** A ground formed of short lengths of twist canes.

Lampwork. Manipulation of glass by means of a gas burner or torch.

Latticinio. A lacy backdrop created from white and clear glass. Whereas "lace" is uniformly chaotic, latticinio is a basketweave pattern. The effect is created by laying white glass rods in a pattern over glass and blowing the mass into a bubble, which is then collapsed.

Letter cane. See **signature cane.**

Making mark. An indentation around the weight where the two halves were put together.

Millefiori. "A thousand flowers" in Italian; the cross sections of molded glass rods of various sizes, colors and patterns.

Muslin. See **lace.**

Paperweight. A glass hemisphere or plaque enclosing decorative elements such as millefiori canes, lampwork motifs of colored glass, sulphide portraits or metallic motifs.

Pastry mold cane. A millefiori cane which flares or "skirts" out at its basal end.

Picture cane. A silhouette cane employing more than one color within the silhouette.

Profile. The shape of a paperweight viewed from the side.

Printy. See **facet.**

Ribbon. A cane containing a flat ribbon-like element, sometimes twisted, used in crown weights, torsades, and chequer weights.

Rock ground (or **sand ground**). A granular, uneven paperweight ground formed with unfused sand, mica flakes, and green glass.

Rod. A cylindrical length of glass, most often containing a simple molded design of more than one color, the basic component of a millefiori cane.

Sand ground. See **rock ground.**

Scrambled millefiori (or **end-of-day weight**). A millefiori paperweight design in which whole or broken canes, and sometimes white or colored "lace," are jumbled together to fill the weights.

Signature cane (or **initial cane,** or **letter cane**). A millefiori cane bearing the name or initial(s) of the weight's factory of origin or the artist who created it.

Silhouette cane. A millefiori cane which in cross-section reveals the silhouette of an animal, flower or figure, in one color.

Sulphide. A three-dimensional ceramic medallion or portrait plaque used as a decorative enclosure in paperweights or other glass objects.

Torsade. A glass ring made of a twist cane, usually found near the base of a mushroom weight.

Twist. White or colored glass threads spiralled around a clear glass rod.

Upset muslin. See **lace.**

Whorl rod. A millefiori cane component with a spiral cross-section. Often used as the center of a cluster of star rods.

Window. A facet on an overlay paperweight.

Paperweight Producers

Producer	Location
Producer	*Location*
Baccarat	Baccarat, France
Bacchus	Birmingham, England
Bohemian factories	Various locations
Clichy	Clichy, France
Gillinder	Philadelphia, Pennsylvania
Islington	Birmingham, England
New England Glass Company (NEGC)	Cambridge, Massachusetts
Sandwich	Sandwich, Massachusetts
Saint Louis	St. Louis les-Bitche, France
Venice	Murano, Italy
Whitefriars	London, England

Bibliography

A Clarke, T. H., Pietro Bigaglia and the Venetian Scientific Congress of 1847; *Annual Bulletin of the Paperweight Collector's Association (1978)*

B Eckel, Lucile and Don, Roses, Roses, Roses; *Annual Bulletin of the Paperweight Collector's Association (1974)*

C Eckel, Lucile and Don, Some Unusual Baccarat Silhouette Canes; *Annual Bulletin of the Paperweight Collector's Association (1975)*

D Hollister, Paul, *The Encyclopedia of Glass Paperweights;* Clarkson N. Potter, Inc., 1969

E Hollister, Paul and Dwight P. Lanmon, *Paperweights: "Flowers which clothe the meadows";* Corning Museum of Glass, 1978

F Kulles, George N., French Millefiori Close-Up; *Annual Bulletin of the Paperweight Collector's Association (1979)*

G McCawley, Patricia K., *Glass Paperweights;* Charles Letts Books Limited, 1975 (revised edition 1982)

H Selman, Lawrence H. and Linda Pope, *Paperweights for Collectors;* Paperweight Press, 1975